PICTUREPEDIA

NOTE TO PARENTS

This book is part of PICTUREPEDIA, a completely
new kind of information series for children.
Its unique combination of pictures and words
encourages children to use their eyes to discover and
explore the world, while introducing them to a wealth
of basic knowledge. Clear, straightforward text
explains each picture thoroughly and provides
additional information about the topic.

'Looking it up' becomes an easy task with
PICTUREPEDIA, an ideal first reference for all types of
schoolwork. Because PICTUREPEDIA is also entertaining,
children will enjoy reading its words and looking
at its pictures over and over again. You can encourage
and stimulate further inquiry by helping your child
pose simple questions for the whole family to
'look up' and answer together.

BIRDS

DK

DORLING KINDERSLEY

LONDON, NEW YORK, AUCKLAND
DELHI, MUNICH, SYDNEY

DK www.dk.com

First published in Great Britain in 1993
by Dorling Kindersley Limited, London

This updated edition published in 2000 by:

Dorling Kindersley Limited
9 Henrietta Street, London WC2E 8PS, Great Britain

Dorling Kindersley Publishing Pty Limited
(A.C.N. 078 414 445)
118-120 Pacific Highway, St Leonards NSW 2065, Australia

Dorling Kindersley (India) Pvt. Ltd.
102/3 Kaushalya Park, Hauz Khas, New Delhi 110016, India

A CIP catalogue record for this
book is available from the British Library.

ISBN 0 7513 6904 7

Reproduction by Colourscan, Singapore
Printed and bound by L. Rex Printing Company Limited, China

BIRDS

A DORLING KINDERSLEY BOOK

CONTENTS

WHAT IS A BIRD?

Any animal that grows feathers is a bird. All birds have feathers, even those species that cannot fly. Like aeroplanes, these feathered flying machines have smooth bodies that can slip through the air. They soar above snowy mountains, dart through steamy jungles and skim over ocean waves. There are more than 100,000 million birds living with us on Earth.

The First Bird

This cat-sized animal, called an archaeopteryx, lived on Earth over 150 million years ago. Like a dinosaur, it had teeth, but it also had feathers – so it was a bird.

Birds have wings instead of arms.

Like you, birds breathe oxygen into their lungs. But birds can also store this flying-fuel in tiny sacs all over their body.

Scaly toes

Birds have a horny beak, and no teeth.

Chewing without Teeth

Birds can't chew their food because they don't have teeth. Instead, they have a special grinding organ called a gizzard. Food is crushed by muscles as it sloshes around the gizzard.

This bulge is a 'storage bag' called a crop. Food stays here and can be coughed up for chicks to eat!

Many birds swallow grit. This stays in the gizzard and helps to grind up food.

Waste will pass out of the body.

Bony Bird

Here is a skeleton of a green-winged parrot. These bones are different to those inside your body – most birds' bones are hollow, like straws. Solid bones would make them too heavy to fly. Even a huge golden eagle weighs less than four kilograms.

Struts criss-cross the inside of the hollow bones to make them strong.

This plate of bone is called a keel. The massive muscles that make the wings flap are fixed to it. Flightless birds do not have a large keel.

Tall and Small

Some birds are bigger than people. Others are almost as small as bees.

The ears are hidden beneath feathers.

A green-winged parrot has more bones in its neck than a giraffe does!

Wood duck

Quetzal

Andean cock-of-the-rock

Hoopoe

Bee hummingbird

King penguin

Look out for us in this book and you will see what size birds really are!

Laughing kookaburra

Greater flamingo

Ostrich

FEATHERS AND FLYING

Feathers are made of keratin, like your hair and nails!

Three types of animal can fly – birds, bats and insects. Birds are the best fliers because they have a coat of feathers. Long, light feathers or small, soft feathers cover almost every part of a bird's body. Usually, only a bird's beak, eyes, legs and feet are bare. Feathers do much more than cover a bird's naked body: they keep birds warm and dry and enable them to stay up in the air.

Ducks fly in a straight line.

Flapping　　*Resting*　　*Scarlet tanagers bob up and down as they flap, then rest, then flap again.*

Flight Patterns
Flying can be hard work. Not all birds flap their wings all the time. Some birds save energy by resting between short bursts of flapping.

Wind Power
If you blow hard across the top of a piece of paper, the air on top moves faster than the air underneath. This difference in air speed creates lift and the paper rises. In a similar way, the air moving over the top of a bird's wing moves faster than the air going underneath it. This lifts the bird up in the sky.

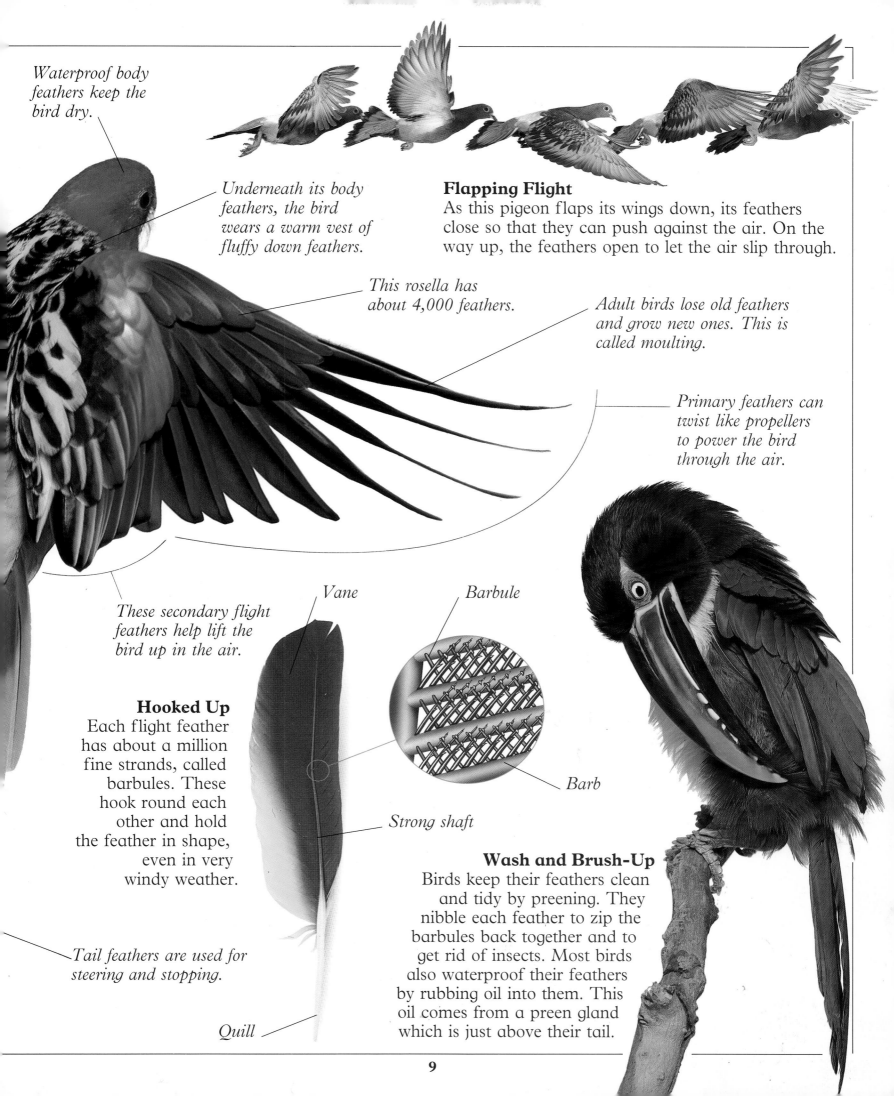

Waterproof body feathers keep the bird dry.

Underneath its body feathers, the bird wears a warm vest of fluffy down feathers.

Flapping Flight
As this pigeon flaps its wings down, its feathers close so that they can push against the air. On the way up, the feathers open to let the air slip through.

This rosella has about 4,000 feathers.

Adult birds lose old feathers and grow new ones. This is called moulting.

Primary feathers can twist like propellers to power the bird through the air.

These secondary flight feathers help lift the bird up in the air.

Vane

Barbule

Hooked Up
Each flight feather has about a million fine strands, called barbules. These hook round each other and hold the feather in shape, even in very windy weather.

Barb

Strong shaft

Tail feathers are used for steering and stopping.

Wash and Brush-Up
Birds keep their feathers clean and tidy by preening. They nibble each feather to zip the barbules back together and to get rid of insects. Most birds also waterproof their feathers by rubbing oil into them. This oil comes from a preen gland which is just above their tail.

Quill

9

SETTING UP HOME

A nest is a cradle in which eggs and baby birds are kept safe from enemies such as snakes and rats. Nests can be holes in trees, mounds of earth or piles of branches. Greenfinches tuck their cup-shaped nests into bushes where they cannot be seen, whereas eagles' lofty nests are easy to see but hard to get at. Each species tries to give its chicks the best chance of survival.

Courting
Before starting a family, male birds have to attract a mate. Peacocks do this by showing off!

Nesting Material
Birds, just like people, build their homes out of all sorts of things. Most nests are made with twigs and leaves, but a few use much stranger ingredients, such as string.

Cattle hair

Seeds

String

Silver foil

Many songbirds glue their nest together with sticky cobwebs!

Birds may make thousands of trips to collect all their nesting material.

Building a Nursery
In many species of bird, both parents build the nest. These long-legged great blue herons are trampling on twigs to make a huge, cup-shaped nest.

Spot the Eggs
Ringed plovers don't build a nest. They lay their pebble-like eggs on the beach.

No Teacher Needed
Weavers are brilliant builders, but they don't have lessons or copy other birds. They just know how to weave their nest. This 'knowing without learning' is called instinct.

Cup-shaped nests have walls to stop eggs from rolling out.

Baby birds don't need pillows – they have soft feathers to lie on.

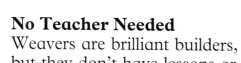

Knitted Nest
The weaver uses his beak and feet to tie the grass into knots!

Grass is sewn into the nest to form a ring.

After weaving the walls, roof and door, he hangs upside down from his home and invites a female to move in.

Nests in trees and bushes are kept dry by the leaves – they form little umbrellas!

Lichen is used to camouflage the nest.

Dried moss helps to keep the eggs warm.

This cup-nest was built by squashing! The greenfinch pressed the material into place with its breast as it spun round in a circle.

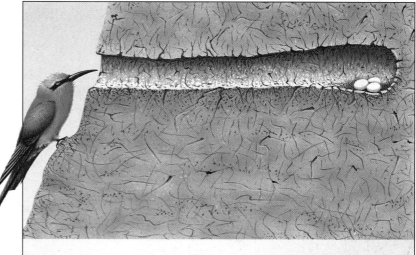

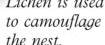

Burrowing Bee-Eater
Carmine bee-eaters nest underground! The male chooses a sandy riverbank and pecks at the earth. When the dent is big enough to cling to, he starts to dig with his beak and feet. The female moves in when all the work is done!

FAMILY LIFE

Family life for most birds is brief, but busy. After the female bird has mated she lays her eggs, usually in a nest. The baby birds, or chicks, do not grow inside her because this would make her far too heavy to fly. When they hatch, the chicks eat a lot, grow bigger and bigger, and then, as soon as they can fly, they leave home for ever.

Baby Sitting
Eggs must be incubated, or kept warm, otherwise the baby birds inside will die. The parents do this by sitting on them.

What's Inside an Egg?
All bird eggs have the same things inside them: a growing baby bird which feeds on a yellow yolk, and a watery egg white which cushions the chick from knocks. Woodpeckers and warblers are ready to hatch in 11 days but Royal albatrosses take more than 11 weeks!

Ostrich egg (actual size)

Hummingbird egg (actual size)

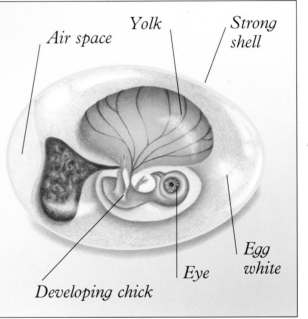

Air space

Yolk

Strong shell

Eye

Egg white

Developing chick

Peck, Peck, Peck . . .
Getting out of an egg is called hatching. The chick taps at the tough shell until it is free. This can take hours or even days!

The blunt end of the egg is pecked off by the chick with a horny spike called an egg-tooth.

First crack

The chick cheeps to tell its parents it is hatching.

Empty shell

Nearly Grown Up
After baby birds have left home they are called fledglings. Many are eaten by cats and hawks, but some from each nest survive and have families of their own.

Feed Me!
Nestlings are helpless when they hatch: they are blind and naked. All they can do is eat and grow.

The parents push food into their chicks' bright, begging beaks.

Fast Food
Blue tits bring back more than 1,000 juicy caterpillars and aphids to the nest each day for their hungry chicks.

Caterpillar

Ducks' eyes are open when they are born.

The wet, sticky fluff, or down, soon dries out.

After the chick has pushed itself head-first out of the egg it is very tired.

Follow the Leader
Baby ducks follow the first big, moving thing that they see – usually one of their parents. This instinct is called imprinting.

This egg-tooth drops off after a few days.

Like most water birds, just one hour after hatching this duckling can walk, see, swim and feed itself.

THE FROZEN NORTH

The North Pole lies in the middle of a frozen ocean, which is surrounded by a cold, flat, treeless, snowy wasteland, called the tundra. Few birds can survive the long, dark winters of the tundra. But in the summer, when the Sun never sets, millions of birds arrive to raise their families. Flowers bloom and the air is full of buzzing insects, but in just a few short weeks the summer holiday is over and they all fly south again.

The Big Melt
During the summer, the ice melts. But this water can't sink into the frozen ground, so it forms lots of lakes – ideal for ducks!

Bird's Eye View

Hunting birds have eyes on the front of their head so that the sight from both eyes overlaps and they can see exactly how far away their victims are. Birds which are eaten by other animals, have eyes on the side of their head, so they can look around for danger.

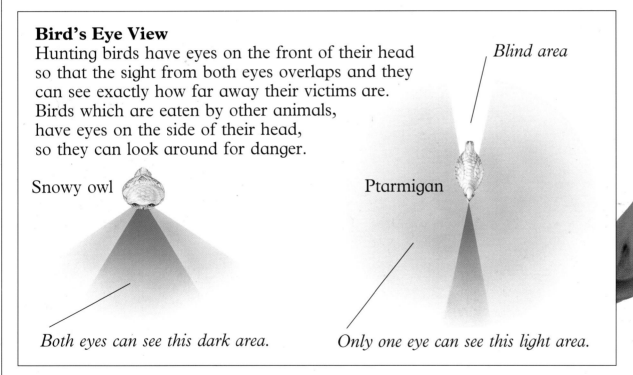

Blind area

Snowy owl

Ptarmigan

Both eyes can see this dark area.

Only one eye can see this light area.

Tundra Residents

Snowy owl

Gyr falcon

Snow bunting

Raven

Tough ptarmigans survive the winter by eating dwarf willow twigs.

Birds have a third eyelid that is see-through and helps keep their eyes moist.

Ptarmigans shiver to keep warm.

Snow-coloured feathers camouflage ptarmigans.

Causing a Stir

Red phalaropes reach the insects that live at the bottom of lakes by swimming in circles! This stirs up the water and makes the insects float upwards. You can try this too – put some buttons in a bowl of water, give it a stir and watch!

Duck Down

Eider ducks pluck soft feathers, called down, from their breast to line their nest. People collect this down to make soft pillows.

Eider down

Summer Coat

Willow ptarmigans don't need thick, white coats in the warm summer, so they moult, and grow dark red feathers.

Just like big, woolly socks, these feathers keep the ptarmigan's legs, feet and toes warm.

Willow ptarmigans are about 35 centimetres tall and live in the Arctic.

Summer Visitors

Ruff

Red phalarope

Red-breasted goose

King eider

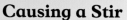

WAY UP HIGH

Long wings help eagles soar.

As you climb a mountain it gets colder and colder. Even if tropical forests grow at the bottom, there can be snow at the top. In between there are bands of woodland, grassland and tundra. Different birds live at every level. Way up high, near the blustery mountain tops, eagles ride the wind and alpine choughs hunt for spiders. Nobody knows how they survive – people need oxygen supplies when they climb this high up.

Playful Polly
The kea is an unusual parrot. It lives high in the mountains and it eats meat as well as fruit.

Keas scream out 'keaaa' as they fly.

Going Up?
Himalayan monals cannot fly very well. They escape from danger by flying downhill – then they have to waddle all the way back up!

Eagles hitch lifts on spirals of warm air, called thermals – it's easier than flapping wings!

Keas love to burst car tyres and pull down campers' tents with their strong claws and beak!

Home Ground
Each pair of big black eagles needs a hunting-ground, or territory, of at least 12 square kilometres to provide enough food for their family. All other eagles are attacked and driven out!

When threatened, eagles scream.

Black eagles live in Africa. Females are usually bigger than males and have a wingspan of more than two metres.

Large eagles have slotted, finger-like wing tips. The feathers spread out to catch the wind and produce more lift.

This bird has dropped one feather. If it moulted all its feathers at once it would not be able to fly.

Eaten by Eagles

Hyrax

Dikdik

Top of the World
After battling against ice, snow and freezing winds, the climbers had nearly reached the top of Mount Everest. And what did they see? Big, black birds called alpine choughs!

When it reaches the top of a thermal, it glides to the base of the next one.

Eyrie

By swooping in and out of the mountain tops, an eagle can sneak up on its prey. The hyrax doesn't see the danger and is swept into the air.

COLD FORESTS

One-tenth of the land on Earth is covered in conifers. These tall trees, such as pines and firs, have needles instead of broad leaves and woody cones instead of flowers. The cold forests are home to many birds, from seed-eating siskins to big birds of prey. But conifer forests planted by people, where the trees are all the same type, height and age, are home to fewer birds.

The siskin's tail spreads out and acts as a brake.

These feathers are called the alula – they are joined to the bird's thumb.

This Japanese waxwing has a bunch of little feathers, called a crest, on its head.

The feet are stretched out to grab the branch.

Sleeping Safely
When birds bend their legs to sit down, or perch, muscles in their legs make their toes curl. Now the bird can't fall off its perch, even if it falls asleep!

Ant Antics
A Steller's jay gets rid of mites or feather lice by making ants crawl all over its body. The ants get annoyed and squirt out formic acid, which kills the tiny insects!

Angry ants

Waxwings are named after these red dots – which look like drops of wax.

Cone-Opener

Crossbills' beaks can snip open cones a bit like a tin-opener. Red crossbills eat spruce seeds, but bigger species can open up large pine cones.

Crossed beak

Larch cone

This greenish-brown bird is a female red crossbill – only the males are red!

Spruce cone

Starved Out

Every few years, winter is even colder than usual. When this happens, the crossbills and waxwings leave the cold forest to feed in warmer woods.

By opening up its feathers, the siskin can reduce its speed.

Pine cone

Inside a Cone

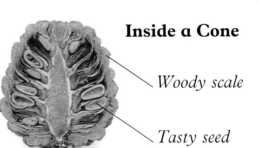

Woody scale

Tasty seed

Touchdown

Birds have to slow down to land, but, just like planes, if they go too slowly they can stall and fall out of the sky. By sticking out their alula, they can change the flow of the wind over their body and avoid crash-landings!

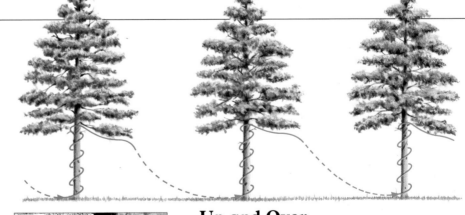

Up and Over

Like a little feathered mouse, the tree creeper creeps up tree trunks looking for spiders and earwigs to eat. It starts at the bottom of the tree, swirls round and round the trunk, walks along the first big branch and then drops down to the bottom of the next tree.

IN THE WOODS

Europe and large parts of America were once covered by a green carpet of trees. Most of these maple, beech and oak woods have been cut down to make room for farms and cities. But if you go into the woods that are left, you may still find some of the beautiful birds that live there. Even if you don't spot them through the layers of leaves, you will hear them. Songbirds, such as nightingales, sing flute-like songs, both day and night.

First-Class Flier
Woodland birds, such as this cheeky blue tit, have short wings. This allows them to twist and turn between the trees.

Woodpeckers' feet are designed for climbing trees – two toes point backwards.

Pied flycatcher chasing flies

Tough beak

Tawny owls sleep during the day. This one is being woken up by birds who think it is roosting too near their nests.

This greater spotted woodpecker has a 'shock absorber' around its brain to stop it from getting hurt when the bird hammers.

Who's There?
Knock, knock – this is the sound a woodpecker makes when it hammers its beak onto a tree to dig out insects!

By placing their long, stiff tail-feathers against the tree trunk, woodpeckers are able to keep steady while they feed.

Song thrushes open up snails by hitting them against rocks.

Robins sing to claim their territory.

All Fall Down

Most woodland trees are deciduous – they lose all their leaves in winter. Before they drop their leaves, a few, like this rowan, grow juicy berries that many woodland birds love to eat.

Big Baby

Cuckoos are lazy. They lay their eggs in other birds' nests and let them do all the hard work.

A cuckoo has laid its big egg in this dunnock's nest.

As soon as the baby cuckoo hatches it pushes all the other eggs out of the nest.

The tiny dunnock keeps feeding the cuckoo chick, even when it grows very big!

Crow's nest

Chaffinch eating a caterpillar

This hungry, crafty magpie is waiting for a chance to steal the wood pigeon's eggs.

Wood pigeon

This sparrowhawk is plucking feathers from a hawfinch it has just caught.

Nuthatch

Woodcock

Hawfinch eating seeds

SWAMPS AND MARSHES

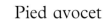

Pied avocet

Half water, half land, swamps and marshes are strange places to live. But to thousands of birds, the shallow water and soggy soil is an ideal home – it is full of food. Birds that live in these tree-filled swamps or murky marshes can either walk through the water or swim. Those that walk, are called waders. Wading birds have long, thin legs, sometimes thinner than a pencil!

To keep their eggs and chicks dry, reed warblers build their nests high up in the reeds, well above the water.

Young scarlet ibises have grey feathers. They only grow red feathers when they are several years old.

Black tip to the long, red wing

This is not a knee, but an ankle!

Highly Strung
Foxes, and other egg-thieves, can't walk on marshy ground. So, to keep their family safe, reed warblers build their homes in tall marsh-plants, called reeds. The nest is tied tightly onto the reeds and won't fall down, even on a windy day.

Scarlet ibises are about 46 centimetres tall and live in swamps in South America.

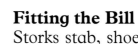

Up in the Air
Walking on stilts makes your legs longer. Now you can splash through puddles and your clothes still won't get wet. A little wading bird, called the black-winged stilt, likes to keep its feathers dry, so it has very, very long legs, which work like stilts.

Fitting the Bill
Storks stab, shoebills dig, flamingos and spoonbills sieve – these amazing beaks, or bills, are all shaped to catch food.

Spoonbill

Nostril

Saddle-billed stock

All birds' legs are covered in small scales.

This long, curved beak can poke deep down into the sticky mud and water at the bottom of the swamp to find frogs and fish.

Shoebill

These big feet stop the ibis sinking into the mud by spreading its weight over a larger area.

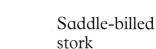

Greater flamingo

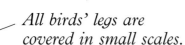

A Shady Bird
Sunlight, shining on water, makes it hard to see the fish below. Black herons solve this problem by shading the water with their wings.

LAKES AND RIVERS

Still lakes and flowing rivers provide a well-stocked larder for flocks of ducks, geese, swans and many more unusual birds. Wherever you live in the world you can spot these wonderful water birds bobbing about on the surface or paddling in the shallows, for they are not shy of people and live on lakes and rivers in cities too.

Flipper Feet
Water birds have webbed feet. They use these webs of skin like flippers, to push through the water.

Splash!
Brilliant blue kingfishers plunge into rivers to catch minnows that are half the length of their body. With its wings folded and its eyes and nostrils tightly shut, the kingfisher flies into the water. It has to struggle to free itself from the pull of the water, but it soon succeeds and flies away with its fish.

Treading Water
These western grebes are dancing. When the birds have paired up, they dance across the lake together. Often a male bird tries to steal another's partner!

Water skiing

Touchdown

Gathering speed

Lift-off

Water-Runways
Heavy water birds can't land or take off on the spot; they need runways like aeroplanes!

Finding Food

Different ducks feed in different ways. Some dabble – they dip their beaks into the water to sieve out tiny plants and animals. Others dive several metres under the water to reach weeds, mussels and insects on the bottom of the lake.

Broad beaks are best for dabbling.

Dabbling ducks never put their whole body under water.

Some diving ducks have notched beaks to hold onto fish.

Shoveler

Teal

Smew

Water Birds

Black swan

Slavonian grebe

Jacana

Ruddy duck

Mallards are about 40 centimetres tall and live all over the world.

It is easy to tell male and female mallards apart – males have green heads.

Water drips off a duck's back because its feathers are waterproof.

Male Mallard

Ducks moult their flight feathers all at once, so for a few weeks each year they can't fly.

Female mallards can quack louder than males.

Female Mallard

Air is trapped between the mallard duck's 12,000 tightly packed feathers to help it float.

These wild mallards may live for 16 years, but most only survive for two or three years.

Webbed foot

SEABIRDS

Playful puffins and graceful gannets, like all seabirds, feed, preen and sleep out at sea for most of the year. But each summer they come ashore to lay their eggs. Most nest in huge groups, called colonies. Their families are safer with thousands of pairs of eyes watching for danger. Some seabirds choose to crowd onto steep cliffs, well out of the reach of many egg-thieves.

These long wings catch the breeze and lift the herring gull up in the air like a kite.

Some seabirds spend most of their life in the air, so they don't often use their legs.

Herring gull chicks peck at this red spot to make their parents cough up food.

Waterproof feathers

Webbed feet

Seabirds do not get tired on long trips because they can glide for hours on end without flapping their wings.

Dive, Dive, Dive!

When a gannet spots a shoal of fish, it folds up its wings and hurtles into the water. Less than ten seconds later, having swallowed the fish under water, it is flying again.

Gannets dive from up to 30 metres into the sea and reach speeds of 100 km/h.

A bony flap covers each nostril.

The hard skull protects the gannet like a crash helmet!

This spear-shaped bill is ideal for stabbing fish.

Floating on Air
When the wind hits a cliff, it shoots up towards the sky. By stretching out their wings, seabirds, such as puffins, can use this breeze to lift them up to their lofty nests.

Beaky Bird
A puffin's big, bright beak is hinged so that it can snap up fish and still keep a grip on those it has already caught.

Puffin

Herring gull

Gannet

Guillemot

Spinning Eggs
Guillemots do not build nests. Their eggs are pointed at one end, so if they are moved they just roll in a circle and not off the cliff.

Going Up!
A cliff is like a high-rise block of flats. Shags nest on the ground floor, in caves near to the bottom of the cliff.

Pebbles that Move
Ringed plovers live on the beach. They are so well camouflaged that they are hard to see.

Shag

S.M

TROPICAL FORESTS

Giant trees, that seem to stretch to the sky, form a huge umbrella over the top of a tropical forest. In the shade beneath this green canopy live thousands of weird and wonderful birds. The hot, wet jungles are home to over half of the world's 9,000 species of birds. Noisy parrots gather fruit and nuts, colourful sunbirds sip the juice out of flowers and harpy eagles swoop down on chattering monkeys.

When a toucan goes to sleep, it rests its big, brightly coloured beak on its back.

Toco toucans are about 35 centimetres tall and live in South America.

This beak is not as heavy as it looks. It is hollow, and has thin rods of bone inside for strength and support.

The toucan uses the jagged edge of its beak like a saw to cut through large fruit.

Big Stretch
With its long, clumsy-looking beak, the toucan can reach fruit and berries that are further away. It picks them and tosses them into its throat.

28

With their strong, hooked beaks, parrots can crack open tough nuts.

Parrots come in all colours. But even bright green ones are hard to spot among tropical fruit and flowers.

Red-fronted parrots are about 25 centimetres tall and live in Africa.

Parrots hold their food with their claws. Some use their right foot and others their left!

This hummingbird's beak is just the right shape to reach to the bottom of the flower.

Fancy Feathers

King of Saxony bird of paradise

Hummingbirds are the only birds that can fly backwards!

Magnificent bird of paradise

Hovering Hummingbird
By flapping their wings very fast, hummingbirds can hover near a flower. They then suck out the flower's juice, or nectar.

Cock-a-Doodle-Doo!
Chickens have been bred from tropical birds, called jungle fowl. These wild birds look and sound very like chickens, but they don't lay as many eggs.

King bird of paradise

White-plumed bird of paradise

GRASSLANDS

Crowned crane

Grass grows in the vast spaces between wet forests and dry deserts. These rolling seas of grass have several names: the tropical African plains are known as savanna and the colder grasslands are called prairies, pampas or steppes. These green lands are important to people because they make good farmland. To birds they are just a perfect place to live. There is tall grass to hide in, and seeds, grasshoppers, beetles and worms waiting to be eaten.

Two for Dinner
Honeyguides love beeswax but they can't open a bees' nest. They have to find a big-clawed badger to rip open the nest for them.

The honeyguide leads the way.

The badger leaves plenty for the patient bird.

Bees

If an oxpecker sees a lion it calls very loudly and warns the buffalo of danger.

Oxpeckers have strong, sharp claws for clinging to thick skin.

Oxpeckers are about 12 centimetres tall and live in Africa.

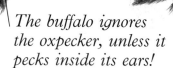

Doctor Oxpecker!
Oxpeckers peck juicy insects, called ticks, out of the skin of buffalo and zebra. This 'surgery' helps to keep the animals healthy.

The buffalo ignores the oxpecker, unless it pecks inside its ears!

Grassland Birds

Western meadowlark

Vulturine guineafowl

Budgerigar

Gouldian finch

Save the Chicken!
Every year there are fewer and fewer prairie chickens living on the American prairies. This is because the grass is being ploughed up and turned into gigantic fields of corn.

Grassland Parrots
Budgerigars are small, green, Australian parrots. In rainy years, there are more 'budgies' in Australia than any other species of bird.

White throat

Bee-Watching Bird
Dainty, white-throated bee-eaters eat most insects but like bees best. When they spot one, they grab it, kill it and swallow it whole!

Hitching a Ride
Kori bustards kick up thousands of insects as they stride through tall grass. Bee-eaters use the bustard as a perch to catch these swarming flies.

The bustard's back is used as a take-off and landing strip!

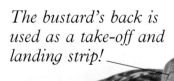

Kori bustards weigh about 23 kilograms!

After killing the bee by thumping it against a branch, the bee-eater closes its beak around the bee and squeezes out the sting.

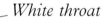

DRY LANDS

At midday, hot, dusty, dry lands are quiet and appear to be empty. Only at sunrise and sunset, when the air and ground are cooler, do birds come out of the shade to feed and find water. Elf owls are lucky – they eat juicy meat and do not need to drink. Sandgrouse eat dry seeds and have to fly up to 50 kilometres every day to get a drink of water.

Sandgrouse Suck
Most birds have to tip their head back to make water trickle down their throat. Sandgrouse are unusual – like you, they can suck.

Shaggy crest

Roadrunners run, but they can also fly.

In cartoons, roadrunners say 'beep beep'! In real life, they rattle their beak to make a 'clack'.

Take-Away Water
Male sandgrouse sit in puddles! Their belly feathers soak up water like sponges. When they return to their nests, the chicks drink from the soggy coat.

After the cold desert night, roadrunners warm up by standing with their backs to the sun and sunbathing.

Roadrunners are about 30 centimetres tall and live in Mexico and North America.

Roadrunners swallow rattlesnakes that are up to 50 centimetres long.

Roadrunners can run as fast as an Olympic sprinter!

Like most ground-feeding birds, roadrunners have long legs and toes.

Roadrunners use their tail to balance as they zig-zag across the desert.

Building a Sand Castle!

A mallee fowl doesn't build a nest, it makes a massive mound. It piles leaves into a pit and covers them with sand. The rotting leaves give out heat and incubate the eggs.

The chicks will dig their way out.

Sand is scraped away if the eggs overheat.

Sandy Birds

Pale-coloured feathers reflect the Sun's heat and are good desert camouflage.

Gila woodpeckers peck away dead bits of cactus as they hunt for insects.

This Western bluebird is keeping cool in a shady bush.

Gambel's quail search under stones for seeds and scorpions.

This little elf owl is sheltering from the scorching sun in a hole made by a gila woodpecker.

Tiny verdin hang upside down from cactus branches to look for insects.

Cactus wrens have scaly legs and tough feathers to protect them from the cactus spines.

THE FROZEN SOUTH

Australia

Antarctica

South Africa

South America

Away from its coasts, Antarctica, the land which surrounds the South Pole, contains almost no life. The blanket of two-kilometre-thick ice, howling winds and freezing temperatures stop plants and land-living animals from surviving. But the ocean around this frozen land is full of fish and krill, so the coasts are home to millions of birds. Penguins are the best known residents of the snowy south but there are also seabirds such as skuas, petrels and terns.

Chinstrap Penguin

Belly Flop
The quickest way to get about on slippery ice is to slide. Penguins can't use a sledge like you, so they scoot along on their big bellies!

Egg-Thief
Skuas rarely go hungry because there are plenty of penguin eggs and chicks for them to steal. While one skua distracts the parent penguins, the other one grabs a meal.

They push themselves along with their strong feet and wings.

These Adélie penguins have to slip and slide over 100 kilometres from their nesting colonies to the sea.

They can't fly, but penguins are excellent swimmers.

Adélies eat small animals called krill.

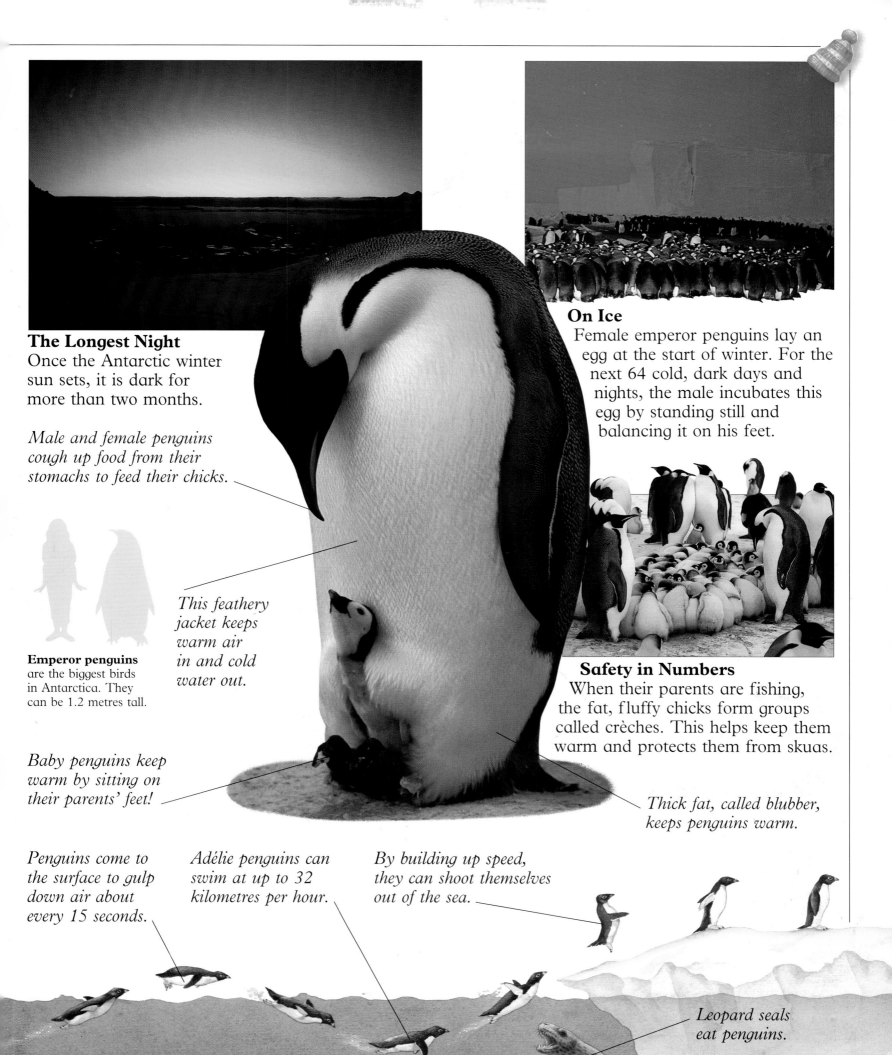

The Longest Night
Once the Antarctic winter sun sets, it is dark for more than two months.

Male and female penguins cough up food from their stomachs to feed their chicks.

Emperor penguins are the biggest birds in Antarctica. They can be 1.2 metres tall.

This feathery jacket keeps warm air in and cold water out.

Baby penguins keep warm by sitting on their parents' feet!

On Ice
Female emperor penguins lay an egg at the start of winter. For the next 64 cold, dark days and nights, the male incubates this egg by standing still and balancing it on his feet.

Safety in Numbers
When their parents are fishing, the fat, fluffy chicks form groups called crèches. This helps keep them warm and protects them from skuas.

Thick fat, called blubber, keeps penguins warm.

Penguins come to the surface to gulp down air about every 15 seconds.

Adélie penguins can swim at up to 32 kilometres per hour.

By building up speed, they can shoot themselves out of the sea.

Leopard seals eat penguins.

BIRDS OF PREY

Eagles, hawks and falcons are birds of prey, or raptors. These strong, fast, fearless birds kill and eat other birds and animals – their prey. Whether they are the size of a sparrow or have a wingspan of three metres, like the condor, they all have three things in common: hooked beaks, sharp claws and 'eagle' eyes that can spot rabbits over five kilometres away!

Dressed for Dinner
Vultures poke their heads into dead animals to eat. Their heads are bare as feathers would get messy!

Steep Stoop
Peregrines have been timed diving at speeds up to 280 kilometres per hour. At the last moment they thrust out their feet and stab their victim with their claws.

Wings are swept back and the tail closes like a fan.

The wings are strong enough to lift the falcon into the air even if it is carrying a dead duck.

Its pointed wings help the peregrine falcon fly faster than any other bird.

Pigeon dies and falls to the ground

The tail is used for steering.

The Biggest Nest in the World
Golden eagles' nests, often called eyries, can be over four metres wide – bigger than some cars! They do not build a new nest every year but fly back to an old nest and just add a few twigs. Some nests are hundreds of years old.

Peregrine falcons
are about 32 centimetres tall and live all over the world.

Bendy Legs!
African harrier hawks have long legs which they use to reach eggs, chicks and bats inside holes in trees. To make it easier to snatch a meal, they can bend their legs backwards, forwards and even sideways.

Working Together
Raptors do not hurt humans and for many hundreds of years, they have been trained to hunt with people. In the Middle Ages, this lanner falcon would have been flown by a squire, a boy who worked for a knight.

The glove stops the bird's claws scratching you.

Meat-Eating Birds

Birds of prey have brilliant colour vision.

Nostril

This powerful, hooked beak is used to pull apart animals that are too big to be swallowed whole.

Like all birds of prey, peregrines spend most of the day resting or preening, not hunting.

Many birds of prey have bare legs, but others wear feathered 'trousers'.

This needle-sharp claw, or talon, is used to grab prey.

American kestrel

Goshawk

All-American Eagle
This US army badge has a bald eagle on it because it is the national bird of the United States.

Harpy eagle

ON THE MOVE

Nearly half the birds on Earth have two homes. In the winter, they leave their summer nesting areas and fly away to warmer places where there will be more food. This year-by-year travelling is called migration. When they migrate, birds tend to fly on one of the three main 'motorways in the sky'. These routes avoid tall mountains and stormy seas. How birds find their way from one side of the world to the other is a mystery. Many people think they are guided by the Sun, Moon, or even by landmarks like hills and rivers.

Safety in Numbers
A large group of birds is called a flock. It is safer flying in a flock because there are more eyes to spot danger.

Follow the Leader
Swirling air slows down large birds. Forming a 'V' pattern in the sky stops this happening – only the leader has to cut through the air.

Swan ring

Owl ring

Cuckoo ring　　Finch ring

Rings on their Legs
You can't ask a bird where it is going, so rings are put around their legs. When a ringed bird is found, you can tell where it has come from.

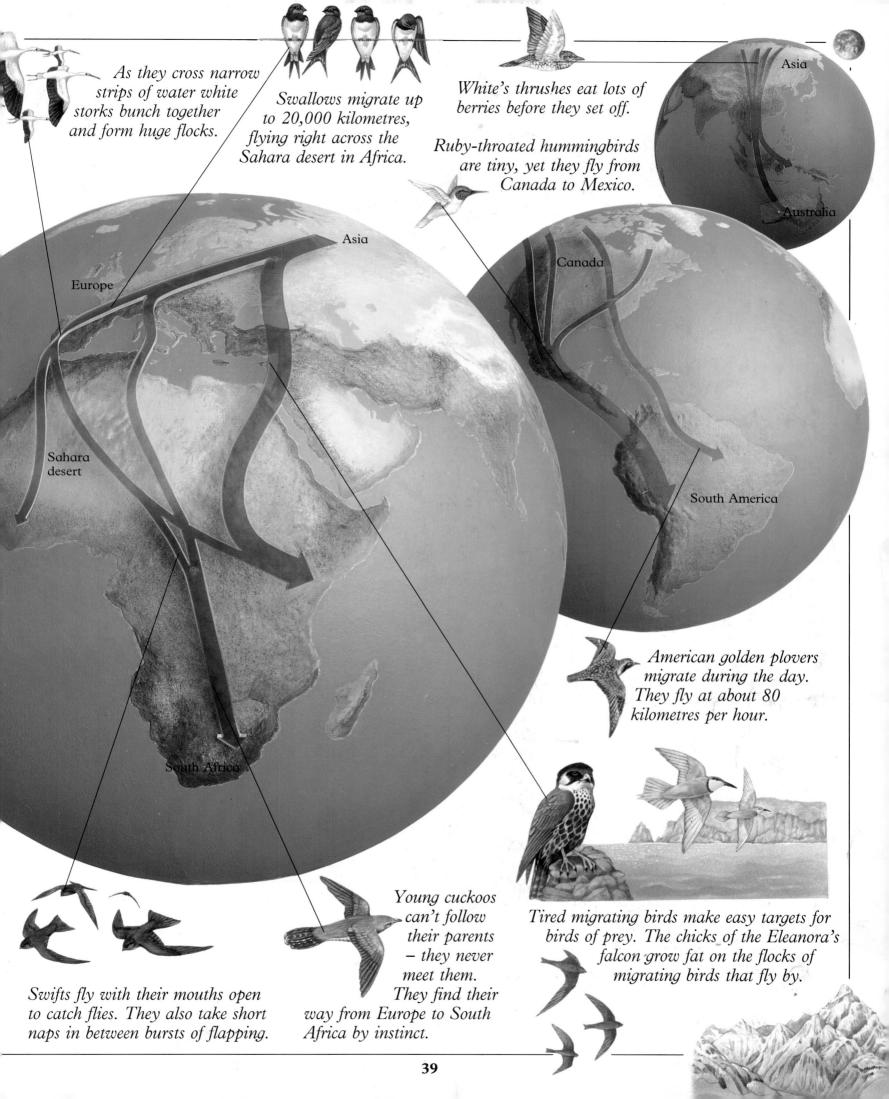

As they cross narrow strips of water white storks bunch together and form huge flocks.

Swallows migrate up to 20,000 kilometres, flying right across the Sahara desert in Africa.

White's thrushes eat lots of berries before they set off.

Ruby-throated hummingbirds are tiny, yet they fly from Canada to Mexico.

Asia

Australia

Asia

Europe

Canada

Sahara desert

South America

South Africa

American golden plovers migrate during the day. They fly at about 80 kilometres per hour.

Young cuckoos can't follow their parents – they never meet them. They find their way from Europe to South Africa by instinct.

Tired migrating birds make easy targets for birds of prey. The chicks of the Eleanora's falcon grow fat on the flocks of migrating birds that fly by.

Swifts fly with their mouths open to catch flies. They also take short naps in between bursts of flapping.

FLIGHTLESS BIRDS

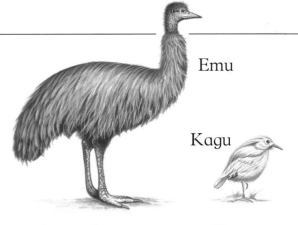

Emu

Kagu

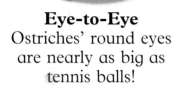

Eye-to-Eye
Ostriches' round eyes are nearly as big as tennis balls!

Flying is hard work – it takes a lot of energy to flap wings and lift off the ground. For most birds it is worth the effort because it helps them escape from danger or search for things to eat. But some birds, like kiwis and kagus, live on islands where there are no enemies and others have found that they can run or swim after food.

Over millions of years, birds such as ostriches, emus and penguins have gradually lost the ability to fly.

Super Egg
Ostriches lay bigger eggs than any other bird: they are 24 times bigger than a chicken's egg! The shell is so strong that even if you stand on top of an ostrich egg, it will not break.

The shell is about two millimetres thick.

Its tiny wings are hidden under brown, fur-like feathers.

The kiwi's nostrils are on the tip of its long beak.

Sniff Sniff
The national bird of New Zealand, the kiwi, is one of only a few birds to have a good sense of smell. It sniffs out worms that are in the soil.

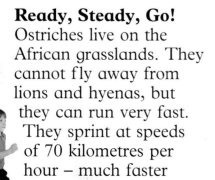

Ready, Steady, Go!
Ostriches live on the African grasslands. They cannot fly away from lions and hyenas, but they can run very fast. They sprint at speeds of 70 kilometres per hour – much faster than a galloping horse.

King penguin

Kakapo

Rhea

Takahe

Brown kiwi

Cassowary

Rheas peck the ground with their big, flat beaks to snap up grass, seeds and leaves.

These frilly feathers keep the rhea warm at night.

By spreading its wings out like a sail, the rhea can catch the wind and run even faster.

Rheas are 1.5 metres tall, weigh more than 20 kilograms and live in South America.

Males wave their skinny, bare necks from side-to-side to attract a female.

Come to Daddy
Rheas are unusual. The males, not the females, incubate the eggs and look after their big babies for up to five months.

Cassowary foot

Ostrich foot

Running birds have massive, muscular legs.

The bones inside this leg are solid. Rheas don't fly, so they do not need lightweight bones.

Rheas look shaggy because the barbules on their feathers do not 'zip together'. Flightless birds do not need neat feathers.

Three front-facing toes.

Running 'Shoes'
The ostrich is the only bird to have two toes; most birds have four toes.

NIGHT BIRDS

As the sun sets most birds settle down to sleep, but some are just waking up. Owls, and other birds that feed and fly in the dark, are called nocturnal birds. They come out at night because there are fewer animals competing for food and many bird-eating eagles are asleep! Owls hoot loudly to one another in the dead of night – they are often heard but seldom seen.

Owls can fly without making a noise because special fringed feathers slow down the air as it rushes over their wings.

Slow, Silent Swoop
In the dark, barn owls use their ears, not their eyes, to find their food. They can even hear a tiny mouse chewing a seed.

Night-Fishing
Waders, like this black-crowned night heron, feed in shallow water. So if the tide is out in the middle of the night, that is when they fish.

Many night birds have dark feathers to help them hide in the dark.

Did you spot this nightjar?

Short tail

Spot the Bird
During the day, nightjars sleep on the ground. Their feathers are the colour of leaves, so if they stay still, foxes and falcons won't find them.

Wooden Actor
If a frogmouth sees you it will point its head up at the sky and pretend to be a broken branch. It leaves one eye slightly open though, just in case you're not fooled.

Owls see ten times better than you in the dark!

Owls cannot move their eyes, but they can turn their necks right round to look backwards.

Like all birds, the ears are small slits hidden under the feathers.

Boobook owls are often called 'morepork' owls – this is what they shout!

Boobook owls are about 20 centimetres tall and live in Australia and New Zealand.

Face to Face

Long-eared owl

Elf owl

Barn owl

Eagle owl

Soft feathers

This curved claw kills rats, mice, lizards and spiders.

Cough it Up
Owls don't have teeth, so they can't chew their food – mice and birds are swallowed whole! Bones, feathers and fur cannot be digested so they are made into pellets and coughed up.

Vole rib

Mouse leg bone

Vole fur

Skull   Hip bones   Jaw   Leg bones   Shoulder blades

BIRDS AND PEOPLE

All over the world, land is being covered with more and more houses, factories, fields and roads. Many species of bird cannot cope with this and they fly away or die out. But some, such as starlings, sparrows and pigeons, have learnt to live with people. Adaptable birds learn to feed in gardens instead of grasslands, nest on tall buildings instead of cliffs and hunt in parks instead of woodlands.

Not Shy
Birds that live near people can become very tame. These house sparrows are eating seeds from someone's hand.

A Welcome Guest
For hundreds of years, people have believed that white storks bring good luck. Villagers in southern Europe put cartwheels on top of their roofs for the storks to nest on.

Down on the Farm
Ploughing destroys many birds' homes, but it helps cattle egrets. These elegant birds love farmland. Over the last 40 years, they have spread right across America and Australia.

Put out fruit, cheese and moist brown bread.

Robins and finches will feed from a bird table.

Blue tits can hang upside down to eat from a coconut.

Thread unsalted peanuts on a string.

Put up a nest box in a quiet corner of the garden.

Garden Birds

You can attract birds to your garden by putting out food. They will eat on the ground but a bird table is better because cats can't leap on top of the feeding birds. If you don't have a garden, you can scatter food on your windowsill.

Home from Home

As long as the site is safe, birds are not fussy where they build their nest. This spotted flycatcher is using an old mincer.

A city bird's main enemies are cats and cars!

House sparrows once lived in woods and ate seeds. In cities they eat our leftovers.

Worldwide

By the mid-19th century, sparrows had spread with people across most of the world. In 1852, a few were set free in New York and in the late 1860's a few more in Australia. They quickly conquered these lands too.

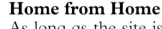

City Birds

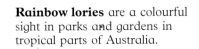

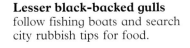

Blue jays live in America. These bossy birds can easily be attracted to bird tables.

Rainbow lories are a colourful sight in parks and gardens in tropical parts of Australia.

Lesser black-backed gulls follow fishing boats and search city rubbish tips for food.

Starlings live all over the world. As the sun sets, they commute into cities to sleep, or roost.

BIRDS IN DANGER

Dodo

Passenger pigeon

Great auk

Imagine a world without robins, penguins or eagles. It could happen! No species of bird is completely free from danger. The passenger pigeon was once the most common bird in the world, but billions were shot and the species became extinct. Flightless birds that live on small islands, like the long-dead dodo, are especially at risk – they can't escape when people fell trees or drain marshes.

Legal Eagle
Thousands of bald eagles have been shot or killed by poisons. They are now protected by law in the USA.

How Birds are Put in Danger

Parrots and macaws are very popular and very expensive. People steal their chicks and eggs to sell.

Many birds are shot by hunters for food, or for sport.

After their home has been chopped down, to make room for cattle to graze, forest birds have nowhere to live, and will die.

Nene geese eat grass. Once they had lots of food, now they have to compete with sheep.

People accidentally brought rats to this island. Many birds can't fight rats and are now in danger.

Pet-Trade Peril
Only one in ten parrots survives being trapped and sent overseas. Over 70 species, such as this St. Vincent's parrot, are now in danger of becoming extinct.

Saved in Time
In 1949, when there were only 50 nene geese left, six were caught and shipped to Britain. They bred so well that hundreds have been sent back to Hawaii.

A Helping Hand
California condors are one of the rarest birds in the world – only about 30 remain, all in captivity. Experts are trying to help them increase in numbers. This chick was hatched in an incubator and is now being fed by a glove puppet that looks like an adult condor.

Sheep eat the bushes in which palilas nest. Now they have nowhere to raise their families.

Hawaiian petrels are rare because cats eat their eggs and chicks.

Kestrels will die if they eat mice that have eaten pesticide-coated seeds.

Farmers spray crops with pesticides. These insect-killing poisons are then washed into the sea.

Pesticides are swallowed by fish, which are eaten by pelicans. The poison makes the pelican's eggshells grow too thin to hatch.

Oil spills kill seabirds.

GLOSSARY

Adapt To change to fit in with new surroundings.

Bill The horny part of a bird's mouth with which it gathers food. It is more often called a beak.

Breeding season The time of year when birds build nests, lay eggs and look after their young.

Brood patch A bald spot on the breast of a bird. The warm, featherless skin helps to incubate eggs.

Camouflage Colours and patterns on feathers help birds to match their surroundings and so to hide from their enemies.

Chick A young bird which has not yet grown its first feathers and begun to fly.

Cliff A steep, high wall of rock on which seabirds nest. Cliffs are often found along the seashore.

Cock A male bird.

Colony A group of birds, of the same species, nesting in one place.

Courtship The way a bird tries to attract a mate to breed with.

Crèche A large group of young birds that gather together for safety.

Desert An area of dry land that has little or no rain.

Egg A hard-shelled, oval or round object that is laid by a female bird. Chicks grow inside an egg until they hatch.

Extinct A species is extinct when all the members of the species are dead.

Feather Flat, light 'frills' that grow over almost all of a bird's body. They keep birds warm and dry, and enable many species to fly.

Fledging The time when a young bird first flies.

Fledgling A bird that has grown its first feathers and begun to fly.

Flight pattern The way a bird moves through the air. Some fly in straight lines, others bob up and down.

Flock A group of birds that moves around together.

Gliding Flying by keeping the wings still and floating on the wind.

Hatching A chick hatches when it breaks out of an egg.

Hen A female bird.

Hovering Staying above one place on the ground by beating the wings.

Incubation Keeping eggs warm, usually by sitting on them, so that the chicks inside will grow and hatch.

Instinct Knowing how to do something without being taught. Birds are born knowing how to build nests by instinct.

Lift The upward force that holds birds up in the air. It is caused by the movement of air over the wings.

Mate The sexual partner of a bird.

Moulting The shedding of old feathers and the growing of new ones.

Nest A safe place to lay eggs and raise a family.

Nocturnal Active during the night and asleep during the day.

Perch A bird's resting place, often a twig.

Plumage The feathers of a bird. Plumage is often more brightly coloured during the breeding season.

Preening When a bird cleans, tidies and oils its feathers with its beak.

Prey The animals that are hunted by raptors and owls.

Roosting Sleeping or resting. A roost is also the place where birds sleep.

Seed The fruit of a plant that many small birds eat.

Species A group of birds that look alike, behave in the same way and can breed together.

Territory The area in which a bird lives. It is defended against intruders.

Thermal A spiral of warm air on which large birds can float upwards.

Wingspan The distance between two wing tips.

Acknowledgments

Photography: Andy Crawford, Steve Gorton, Cyril Laubscher, Tim Ridley, James Stevenson and Jerry Young.

Illustrations: Sandra Doyle, Roy Flooks, Mick Gillah, Edwina Hannah, Stuart Lafford, Mick Loates, Sean Milne and John Searl.

Models: Donks Models.

Thanks to: Eddie Hare at the Raptor Centre in Chilham, Kent and Truly Scrumptious Child Model Agency.

Picture credits

Doug Allen: 35 bl & br; **Aquila Photographics:** Conrad Greaves 23t; **Ardea:** G. K. Brown 33r, Kenneth W. Fink 47l, A. Greensmith 44r, John Swedberg 26; **Biofotos:** Paul Ormerod 38t; **Bruce Coleman Ltd.:** Jen & Des Bartlett 32l, Erwin & Peggy Bauer 31r, Jane Burton 6, David Chouston 36t, Francisco Erize 34t, Jeff Foott 32r, Frances Furlong 26t, Dennis Green 12, 45, Frank Greenaway 27t, Gordon Langsbury 27bl, Hans Reinhard 1, 16, John Shaw 18/19, Joseph Van Wormer 47r; **Comstock Inc.:** George Lepp 12/13; **FLPA:** M. Newman 14/15, Fritz Polking 30, Len Robinson 43; **Jacana:** Jean-Michel Labat 11, Jean-Philippe Varin 13t; **Nature Photographers Ltd.:** Frank Blackburn 36b, Kevin Carlson 22b, Hugh Clark 19, Andrew Cleave 27br, Ernie Janes 23b, Roger Tidman 20; **NHPA:** N. Dennis 40t, Hellio & Van Ingen 38b, L. H. Newman 31l, John Shaw 15, 46, Roger Tidman 13b, Dave Watts 34b, Martin Wendler 41; **Oxford Scientific Films:** Doug Allen 35tr, G. Bernard 28, J. C. Cannon 35tl, John Downer 17, Michael Leach 3, 44, James H. Robinson 10, Ronald Toms 33l; **Planet Earth Pictures:** Nick Greaves endpapers, Richard Coomber 22t; **Survival Anglia:** Jen & Des Bartlett 40b; **Keith A. Szafranski:** 24tr; **ZEFA:** 14, 26/27, 40c, Heintgel 24tl, tc, & b; **Zoological Society of San Diego:** Ron Garrison 47c.

t – **top**	b – **bottom**	l – **left**	r – **right**	c – **centre**
tl – **top left**	tr – **top right**	tc – **top centre**	bl – **bottom left**	

INDEX